Robert S. Taylor

The Improvement of the Mississippi River

An address delivered at St. Louis, January 26, 1884

Robert S. Taylor

The Improvement of the Mississippi River
An address delivered at St. Louis, January 26, 1884

ISBN/EAN: 9783337302290

Printed in Europe, USA, Canada, Australia, Japan

Cover: Foto ©Andreas Hilbeck / pixelio.de

More available books at **www.hansebooks.com**

THE IMPROVEMENT

—OF THE—

MISSISSIPPI RIVER.

———

AN ADDRESS DELIVERED AT ST. LOUIS,

JANUARY 26, 1884,

—AND—

TWO ARTICLES ORIGINALLY PUBLISHED

—IN THE—

NORTH AMERICAN REVIEW,

-BY-

ROBERT S. TAYLOR,

OF THE MISSISSIPPI RIVER COMMISSION.

——— · ———

REPRINTED BY THE

MISSISSIPPI RIVER IMPROVEMENT COMMITTEE

OF THE

MERCHANTS' EXCHANGE OF ST. LOUIS

THE IMPROVEMENT

—OF THE—

MISSISSIPPI RIVER.

AN ADDRESS DELIVERED AT ST. LOUIS,

JANUARY 26, 1884,

—AND—

TWO ARTICLES ORIGINALLY PUBLISHED

—IN THE—

NORTH AMERICAN REVIEW,

·-BY—

ROBERT S. TAYLOR,

OF THE MISSISSIPPI RIVER COMMISSION.

REPRINTED BY THE

MISSISSIPPI RIVER IMPROVEMENT COMMITTEE

OF THE

MERCHANTS' EXCHANGE OF ST. LOUIS

MAP OF
LOWER MISSISSIPPI
MISSISSIPPI RIVER

SCALE 1:3200000

AUTHORITIES

Mississippi River reduced from Surveys
of Miss. River Commission and Coast Survey.
Alluvial Region from Plate II. Humphreys
and Abbot's Report.

NOTE.

The shaded area denotes lands
subject to overflow.

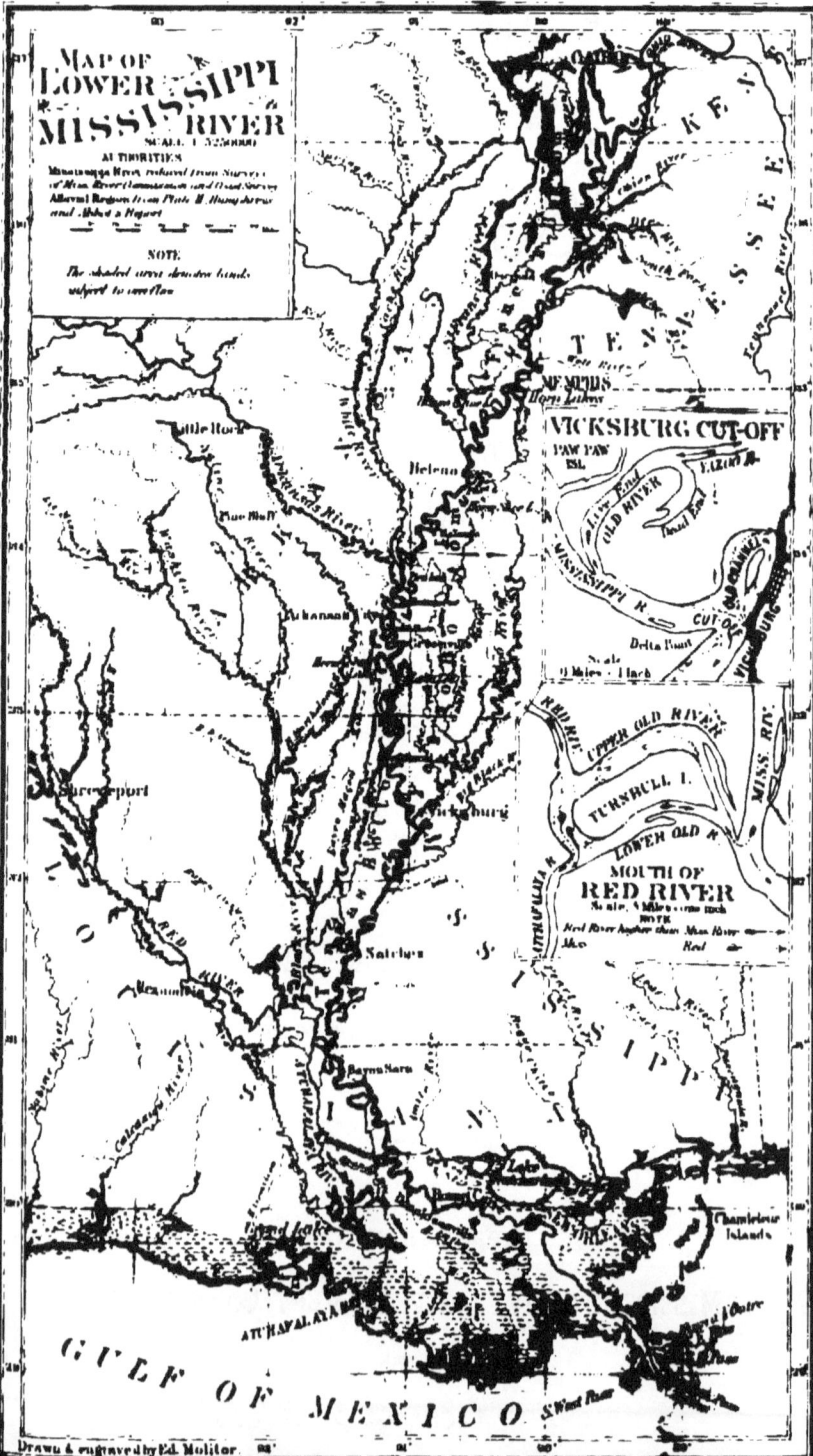

VICKSBURG CUT-OFF

PAW PAW
ISL.

OLD RIVER

MISSISSIPPI R.

CUT-OFF

Delta Point

Scale
5 Miles = 1 Inch

UPPER OLD RIVER

TURNBULL I.

LOWER OLD R.

MOUTH OF
RED RIVER

Scale 4 Miles = one Inch

NOTE

Red River higher than Miss River

TENNESSEE

Memphis

Little Rock

Helena

Pine Bluff

Arkansas

Vicksburg

Shreveport

Natchez

Alexandria

Baton Rouge

Grand Lake

ATCHAFALAYA

New Orleans

Chandeleur
Islands

GULF OF MEXICO

Drawn & engraved by Ed. Molitor.

INTRODUCTORY.

The Mississippi River Improvement Committee of the Merchants' Exchange of St. Louis present to the public in this form the following papers, in the belief that they will be found of value to those who care to understand the theoretical principles and practical methods adopted by the Mississippi River Commission in the work of improving the Mississippi River. This undertaking is by far the most important work of internal improvement ever entered upon by the Government. Its friends feel that it needs only to be thoroughly understood to be assured of the cordial and unanimous support of the public. They have no desire that its difficulty shall be under-estimated ; and they are sure that its value, if successfully accomplished, can not be over-estimated. It is a noble experiment in the interest of all the people;—one wisely undertaken and well begun, and in the final success of which every patriotic citizen ought to feel a personal pride.

In the address here reproduced is given a detailed account of the practical work of the Commission, and of the results so far reached. In the two papers taken, by permission of the publisher, from the *North American Review*, are discussed the two great theoretical topics of Outlets and Levees. These three papers were originally given to the public separately, and contain some repetitions of substantially identical matters. But as these are not numerous, and consist, either of brief statements of fundamental principles, or of facts used in different connections to illustrate different propositions, it has been thought best to reprint each paper entire.

It is desired that every person to whom this publication shall come shall consider that it has been sent to him because he is supposed to be one of those intelligent, liberal-minded citizens to whom all things that concern the welfare of the Republic or any part of it, whether near or far, are of interest, and in the hope that he may be gratified by the perusal of it.

IMPROVEMENT OF THE MISSISSIPPI.

An Address delivered at St. Louis, January 26, 1884, before the Merchants' Exchange.

I have accepted with pleasure your invitation to speak on the subject of the work, proposed and accomplished, of the Mississippi River Commission. It is to be regretted, but nevertheless is true, as your committee have remarked, that information on this subject is not within easy reach of the general public. The commission itself speaks only through its official reports, which are accessible to but few, and which, from their necessarily formal and technical character, are not very inviting reading when obtained. And the nature and situation of the works in progress are such that they are practically beyond the reach, even of the indefatigable newspaper reporter. The undertaking is one of great importance, great difficulty, and great cost. Its successful completion will be impossible without the intelligent and cordial support of the people. And I am glad, therefore, of an opportunity like this, to lay before the public in an informal and familiar way some account of the plans adopted and progress made. I may say, too, that it gives me peculiar gratification to do this here, in the central metropolis of the empire valley, whose citizens have distinguished themselves in many noble works, and preeminently as early and steadfast friends of Mississippi River Improvement.

The first duty imposed on the Mississippi River Commission by the law creating it was, in the language of the Act, "to "direct and complete such surveys of said river between the

"head of the Passes near its mouth to its head waters as may
"now be in progress, and to make such additional surveys,
"examinations, and investigations, topographical, hydro-
"graphical, and hydrometrical of said river and its tributaries
"as may be deemed necessary by said commission to carry
"out the objects of this act."

It is to this part of the work of the commission that I will
invite your attention first. It was surprising information to
me, and I think will be to most persons, that prior to the
present undertaking, no complete survey of the Mississippi
river had been made. The Coast Survey had carried its
work to a distance of about one hundred and sixty-eight miles
from the mouth of the river upward. A stretch of about forty
miles in the vicinity of Memphis, and another of about ten
miles in the vicinity of Cairo had been surveyed under the direction of Gen. C. B. Comstock, now President of the commis-
mission. These surveys have been adopted by the commission as part of its general system. Portions of the upper river
had been surveyed by Col. Farquhar and Maj. Mackenzie, of
the Engineer corps, but the work, though excellent in its execution, was not adapted to the plan fixed upon for the whole,
and will not be used. So that excepting about two hundred
and eighteen miles of the lower river, the survey undertaken
and in progress is a new and complete one, reaching from one
end of the river to the other.

The work of surveying proper comprises three successive
operations, conducted by distinct parties, viz.:

1. Triangulation ;
2. Precise Levelling ;
3. Topography and Hydrography.

The process of triangulation consists in laying out on the
river banks a series of triangles, with sides crossing the river
at intervals of a mile or two, in a zigzag line, like the panels of
a rail fence. Each of these triangles has a side in common
with one preceding it and another with one following it. The
angles being determined by instrumental observation, and one

side of one of the triangles measured as a base, the others are ascertained by computation. The observations and measurements are made with the greatest care and skill, the computation is pure mathematics, and the results are practically exact. The system of lines and stations thus established constitutes the frame upon which all following work is built, and is now complete from the gulf to Keokuk, Iowa.

The system of levelling adopted is equally thorough and exact. Beginning at the Gulf of Mexico, a continuous line is carried up the river, every portion of which is covered by at least two independent observations. No work is accepted which shows a disagreement between two observations, exceeding five millimeters into the square root of the distance in kilometers, or about two-fifths of an inch in seven miles, and, as a rule, the observations agree much more nearly than that. At intervals of three miles transverse lines are located across the river, and in each of these lines are placed four bench-marks,—two on each side of the river. These bench-marks are the permanent monuments of the whole survey. The triangulation stations, being necessarily near the river bank, are difficult to preserve. The bench-marks may be placed wherever the most secure location can be found. They are connected by exact measurements of distance and bearing with the triangulation stations, and thus become at once monuments of distance and elevation. There being four of them in each transverse line, three of each set might be lost without serious inconvenience. Every possible precaution is taken, however, to insure the permanence of every one of them. Wherever bedrock, stone abutments, or stone foundations under public buildings can be found, they are used. In such cases a deep hole is drilled in the rock, in which a copper plug is securely fastened. Upon its surface two lines are engraved, the intersection of which is the point of reference. Such facilities as these for the location of monuments are, however, comparatively rare, and in most cases artificial monuments are used. A brief description of these will not be without interest. The transverse lines before mentioned are extended from one to two miles from the bank on each side, and a bench-mark station is located at each end of the line, and one at an intermediate point on each side of the river. At each of these stations a thick stone slab, some eighteen inches square, is buried about five feet deep, having a cross cut on its upper surface. The intersection of the lines of that cross is the reference point for distances, and the surface of the slab, at the same point, the reference plane for elevations. Directly over this point is set an iron tube, six inches in diameter and six feet long, securely covered by an iron cap, which terminates in a knob, the exact elevation of whose upper surface above the surface of the slab below is known. The visible monument is, therefore, an iron knob surmounting a little mound of earth about a foot high, and for ordinary purposes reference is made to this; but when greater exactness is required, the cap is removed and reference made to the stone below. This part of the work is now complete from the gulf to Savannah, Illinois, a point about fifty miles north of Rock Island. From the latter place a line has been run to Chicago, where it connects with a system of levels brought by other government surveys from the Atlantic ocean by way of the Hudson river and the great lakes. It is impossible to make an exact comparison of results at this time, because the mean tide level of the Gulf of Mexico, upon which the Mississippi levels rest, has not yet been finally fixed by the Coast Survey or other authority. But, taking it as it has been assumed to be in the work done by the commission, the disagreement between the two lines thus meeting in Chicago is less than twelve inches.

The topographical or hydrographical work is last in order, and comprises under the head of topography, the determination of the outlines of the river's banks, bars, and islands, and the contour of adjacent lands for a distance of from one to three miles on each side; and, under the head of hydrography, the determination of the width, depth, boundaries, and shape of the water channel,—all which are referred, both in respect to distance and elevation, to the bench-marks already described. This part of the work is now substantially complete from Cairo to the gulf.

From these surveys are drawn maps upon a scale of about six inches to the mile, upon which are shown all the triangulation stations, bench-marks, soundings, water lines, bars, islands, and other physical features of the surface surveyed. This work is done upon sheets 28 inches wide, and from 40 to 48 inches in length, and is substantially similar to that done by the Coast Survey. These maps exist only in the original manuscript. For practical use they are reproduced and printed in two reduced sizes. The larger of these is upon a scale of about three inches to the mile, and is upon sheets 23x36 inches, and is adapted to use of engineers, public libraries and offices, and other purposes requiring a high degree of minute exactness. Of these maps two sheets, out of a total series of eighty-five, have been published. The smaller reproduction is upon a scale of one inch to the mile, and is intended to meet the wants of pilots, shippers, and the public generally. From these many of the details embraced in the larger maps are necessarily omitted. The number published is twenty-two, and with ten more the series will be complete from Cairo down. It is also in contemplation to publish a large wall map exhibiting the river from Cairo to the gulf on one sheet.

From this brief account of it, it will be seen that the survey in progress is designed, not only to furnish full and exact information for present use, but to perpetuate that information through all time. A very little care will preserve all the monuments of it intact. But even with the grossest inattention they can not be wholly lost. The caving of a bank may occasionally expose a bench-mark to untimely resurrection, but enough of them will remain until Gabriel blows his trump to enable an engineer to reconstruct the river channel exactly as it lay when the survey was made. If it shall wander away from under the worm fence of triangles which the engineers have built upon it, we shall have the proof and measure of its shifting. We shall know whether it fills up its bed, or scours it out, and how much.

Besides these operations of surveying and map making, there are conducted numerous observations comprised under the general term " hydrometrical," which are scarcely less important. At selected stations on the river parties are placed whose duty it is to measure and record daily the depth, width, vertical area, velocity, and discharge of the water; the fill, scour, and other changes of the bottom; and the amount and character of sediment carried in suspension. From the data thus obtained sheets are prepared, on which those functions of the river which it is desirable to compare with others are represented by lines. Thus, one line represents the stage, and curves this way or that, as the river rose or fell. Another line represents the velocity, and curves in this direction or that, as the velocity of the current increased or diminished. Another line represents the vertical water area or cross-section; another the discharge per second, and so on. These lines being placed side by side on the same sheet, the whole can be seen at once, and there is thus exhibited a chart, or pictorial history of the river at the locality observed, by means of which its various functions can be compared, one with another, with an accuracy otherwise impossible. There is also maintained in connection with the Engineer Office at Washington, a system of gauges at intervals of about fifty miles over the river, at each of which a daily record of the stage is kept. Measurements have been made also, of the discharge of the Ohio, and of the overflow discharge of the main river during the great floods of 1882 and 1883.

In order to throw light on the history and character of the alluvial basin, an extensive series of deep borings has been made, the results of which have been submitted to the study of distinguished geologists. And in order to determine the elevations and other features of the great sub-basins, transalluvial lines of levels have been carried across the entire valley at several places.

The object of all this miscellaneous work is not the mere gratification of scientific curiosity, but to provide indispensable material for practical investigation. As will be more fully explained hereafter, there is no possibility of improving the Mississippi river except through the wise directioi. of its own forces. This requires an intimate and accurate knowledge of its history, life, laws, and methods, which can be obtained only by minute, patient and intelligent observation. There has been much discussion of subjects pertaining to the Mississippi river which has been comparatively profitless, for want of authenticated facts. Such observations as I have mentioned, continued systematically and long enough, will furnish those facts, and put at rest questions which might otherwise be discussed forever. Of the truth of this remark, I can give you at this moment a recent and interesting illustration.

The effect of outlets upon the flood levels and upon the river channel has been the theme of great controversy for a generation past. There is a class of aquatic doctors who regard the Mississippi in every time of flood as sick, whose diagnosis of the case is dropsy, and whose remedy is tapping. Bills have been introduced in Congress, and vigorously pushed, to provide for the making of vast outlets by artificial means. The opponents of such measures have claimed that the effect of such diminution of volume in the river is, to lessen its energy and transporting power, and so cause deposits of sediment, which choke up the channel, increase the flood hights, and thus make the last state of the river worse than its first. These views have been supported by many observed facts, and by what seemed to be unanswerable reasoning. Nevertheless, there has been felt by intelligent students of the question a strong desire for more facts, and for facts based on observations so taken as to afford the highest possible guaranty of their accuracy. Some such facts we are now able to give.

During the great flood of 1882, a number of crevasses occurred below Memphis. Less than three months prior to that time a survey of that part of the river had been completed, so that we know its exact depth, width and cross-section at those points as they were before the flood. After the flood a re-survey was ordered to be made in the locality of four of those crevasses, for the express purpose of ascertaining what change, if any, they had produced in the river channel. The results were as follows: at Malone's Landing, where the upper and least crevasse of the four occurred, there was a shoaling of the channel below the crevasse amounting to four per cent. of its cross-section; at Riverton there was a shoaling of fourteen per cent.; at Bolivar, eleven per cent.; and at Mound Place, twenty-four per cent.

At Bonnet Carre, a few miles above New Orleans, a crevasse occurred a number of years ago, through which a large volume of water escaped into Lake Pontchartrain. It remained open until the autumn of 1882, when it was closed. We had a survey of the river adjacent to this crevasse, made before its closure, and have just completed another made since. A comparison of the two shows that since the closure of the crevasse the channel space in the river below it has increased about twelve per cent. We have, therefore, in four cases, a filling up of the river bed following an outflow through a crevasse, and in one, a scouring out of the bed following the closure of a crevasse and the stoppage of its discharge. I am not now arguing the outlet question, and will not take time to comment on the significance of these facts; but that they weigh more than a foolscap quire of conjecture, will be readily admitted.

I have dwelt at some length on this part of the work of the commission, partly because of its own interest and importance, and partly because it has attracted less attention, and is, as I believe, less well understood, than those parts of the work involving larger expenditures. It is, in truth, a work of great and enduring value, not only as a necessary preliminary to any intelligent attempt toward improvement of the river, but as an independent undertaking, national in its scope, and of such usefulness to science, commerce, and public interests, as to justify all the expense necessary to carry on and complete it. It has been, and is, the purpose of the members of the commission to observe and perpetuate for the information of others, so far as the means at their disposal will allow, every fact in the life of the Mississippi river that will help to an accurate understanding of those immutable laws to which, beyond doubt, it is as submissive and obedient as is the rivulet that trickles down the roadside to the laws of its existence and flow. They may fail to interpret their own observations aright, and all their plans for the improvement of the river may go awry, like other plans of mice and men : but, if so, the record of their failure will serve to point out the road to success for those who shall follow.

The other and harder duty imposed upon the commission was, in the words of the Act, "to take into consideration and "mature such plan or plans and estimates as will correct, "permanently locate, and deepen the channel and protect the "banks of the Mississippi river ; improve and give safety and "ease to the navigation thereof; prevent destructive floods ; "and promote and facilitate commerce, trade, and the postal "service." In pursuance of this requirement a plan for the improvement of the river as a highway of navigation has been prepared, reported, approved, and is now in course of execution. The work is done by the Secretary of War through officers of the Engineer corps of the army, who proceed according to the plans, and under the general supervision of the commission, as to the things to be done, and methods to be employed, but whose contracts, disbursements, and accounts are subject to the supervision and approval of the Chief of Engineers. And to some account of those plans, and the work so far done under them, I now invite your attention ; and in that connection will speak, first, of the nature of the obstacles to be overcome ; then of the methods employed ; and finally, of the progress made.

If the Mississippi river could be emptied of its contents, so as to expose its bottom dry and bare, the appearance presented would be surprising to most of us. Instead of a comparatively level channel floor, corresponding in its general features with the lands adjacent to the river, there would be found a succession of great sand hills and intervening depressions. Passing through one of these depressions, the observer would find himself, it might be, a hundred and fifty feet below the surface of the banks on either side. Within a few thousand feet he would encounter a sand hill, stretching across the channel, so steep that you could scarcely drive a horse up its declivity, and perhaps a hundred feet high. Having crossed the top of this, he would descend into another basin, then climb another hill, and so on. When the channel is filled with water the crests of these elevations approach the surface, and so constitute the bars so often mentioned in this connection. In low water the greatest depth above them is sometimes as little as five feet, and often only six or seven. This is insufficient for profitable navigation upon a scale adequate to the growing demands of commerce. To increase that depth is the improvement desired.

There is an elevation of the bottom, and in that sense a bar, below every bend in the river. But most of them are so deeply submerged that they are far below a steamboat keel, even at low water. The number of those that obstruct navigation below Cairo is not far from forty. Nearly all of these are located in groups, each group being comprised in a stretch of river somewhere from twenty to forty miles in length. Such a portion of the river is known in engineering vernacular as a "reach." Of such divisions there are in the lower river six, known as the New Madrid, Plum Point, Memphis, Helena, Choctaw, and Lake Providence reaches. A ten feet low water channel from Cairo down is the least depth that will answer the needs of commerce; the actual demand is fifteen; the ultimate hope twenty. To get ten feet we must scalp from three to five feet off the top of each of the forty sand hills which I have described : to get fifteen, from eight to ten. To do this so that it shall stay done is the whole problem of Mississippi river improvement. Is such a thing possible?

The feature which I have mentioned, of alternate pool and bar, is as invariably characteristic of every alluvial stream as its lateral crookedness. There is thus indicated a law which is universal, by which every such stream tends to make for itself a pathway combining both lateral and vertical curves. Every attempt, therefore, to straighten such a channel in either respect, is, to some extent, a contradiction of the laws that govern the flow of the stream. In regard to such interferences the Father of Waters has a will of his own, which is not to be violently antagonized. And if it were necessary, in order to get a ten or fifteen feet channel, to bring the river bottom to a straight line, or anything like it, I should regard the task as impossible. But that is not necessary, and herein lies the hopefulness of the undertaking. To take ten feet off a sand pile a hundred feet high, is not in itself a problem to discourage an engineer, and it does not very greatly alter the shape or proportions of the river bed. It still leaves the crest of the bar from eighty to ninety feet above the bottom of the pool, which, one would think, ought to satisfy any reasonable river. In fact that depth of bottom curvature does satisfy the Mississippi river throughout most of its course. It is only where disturbing conditions exist, that a greater curvature is found. Hence it seems probable, that, upon the removal or amelioration of those disturbing conditions, the river may submit quietly to the comparatively slight alteration of its present pathway which is necessary for its improvement.

With respect to the means by which the improvement proposed is to be attempted, it may be said in the first place, that the forces to be employed must be found in the river itself. None can be found elsewhere adequate to the occasion. The power of the river to pile sand on its bars is beyond all power of man to remove it. It would be as impossible to make and maintain a fifteen feet channel through the bars by digging or dredging, as to lower a flood by carting away the water.

At the same time, there are forces in the river powerful enough to do the work needed, if they can be put at it. The present channel is the river's own handiwork. Over three-fourths of its course it is good enough. In those places where the channel is bad, the energy of the river is no less than in the places where it is good, but is not well directed. And if the river can be induced to make as economical and effective use of its powers throughout its course as it now makes over the greater part of it, there will be a good channel from Cairo to New Orleans.

It follows that the engineer who would qualify himself for this great work must take the river as his teacher, and sit at its feet, a patient, observant, receptive, reflecting pupil. In these diligent studies every bend, every bar, every willow on the shore will have for him its lesson and its suggestion. And when he shall have learned the secret of the river's success where it succeeds, and of its failure where it fails, he will be prepared to remedy the failure by introducing, so far as may be done, the conditions of the success.

The plan which has been adopted proposes, first, to deepen the channel over the crests of the bars by reducing its low water width at those places. This is a simple imitation of the river's own engineering. Its narrow reaches are always deep; its shallow bars are always wide. The reason for the difference is obvious. A concentration of the current increases its velocity, momentum, and scouring power, and so results in increased depth. As a rule, the shallow reaches also contain islands and bars which subdivide the channel. To choose from the existing subdivisions the one most suitable in its location and dimensions to serve as the main channel, regulate it to a width of from three thousand to thirty-five hundred feet, and close all others, is usually the substance of the project at such a place.

For the closure of chutes and subsidiary channels, and the building of new banks where needed in order to contract the •new channel, the sediment carried in the water is the sole reliance. The conditions of sedimentary deposit are, first, that water loaded with sediment shall flow upon and cover the area to be filled ; second, that it shall there experience such diminution of velocity as to cause the heavier particles to fall to the bottom ; and third, that it shall then flow away and give place to a fresh supply of silt-laden water. The second-ditions exist naturally on the wood and vine covered banks of the river, and are produced artificially by driving piles in rows across the chute or channel, or around and across the space to be filled, and interweaving a wattling of poles and brush among the piles, or placing against them mattresses made of poles and brush, and thus forming a permeable dam or screen, by which the flow of the water is obstructed and delayed, but not prevented. It is desirable that the obstruction presented by these dikes shall be sufficient to diminish the velocity of the water passing through them to such degree as to cause rapid deposit, and yet admit the passage of the largest amount of water consistent with such diminution. These piles and their wattling or mattresses are not intended to serve any permanent use. When the deposit which they are designed to produce is complete, their functions are ended, like those of the scaffolding about a house, when the house is finished. This should not require more than two or three seasons at the utmost. When the deposit caused by them has been carried somewhat above the ordinary low water line, there shortly springs up upon it a spontaneous growth of willows, which take the place of piles and mattresses as checks to the flow of the water, and so carry the deposit higher and higher, until it reaches the normal bank height of the locality.

It is occasionally necessary to narrow the channel selected as the permanent one by the creation of a new bank alongside it. But such cases are comparatively rare. Where the whole river flows in a single channel, there is rarely any serious bar obstruction. Hence, the work of contraction consists chiefly in closing chutes.

The river being by these means deflected from its erratic

and wasteful courses, and led along one symmetrical channel, speedily scours out and deepens its bed to the extent necessary to convey its concentrated volume. This gives the additional depth, which is the improvement sought. If this depth could be obtained and maintained by contraction alone, the works which I have described would be all that would be needed. It is impossible, however, to give complete and permanent effect to this part of the work without protecting the caving banks in the reaches to be improved, and for some distance above them. The Mississippi River, as every one knows, is a succession of bends. In these the current always tends to hug the concave bank. In order to do this it is compelled to cross the channel every time it passes from one bend to another. The points at which these transitions of the current from one side of the river to the other occur are called "crossings." The current swings round the bends with greater velocity than it passes over the crossings. The caving banks are on the concave sides of the bends. As the swift high water current sweeps past them, it gathers up a load of sand, a large part of which it drops on the next crossing below, where its velocity is first slackened. Hence it is, that the bad bars are usually at the crossings below caving bends. And one object, therefore, of protecting such banks is, to prevent the filling up of the deepened channels below them. But the great object of bank protection is to secure a permanent location of the channel. The caving back of a concave bank not only shifts the line of the current where the caving occurs, but changes its location and direction at the crossing below, and so the point and direction of its impingement on the opposite bank. This introduces changes in the bend below, and these others in the next one, and so on down the river. In this way a change in one bend may produce changes in half a dozen bends below it.

One of the resources of the skillful engineer is to avail himself, in certain cases, of this ricochet or rebounding of the current from one bank to the other, by placing his works some distance above the point where their results are to be developed, somewhat after the fashion of a stroke in billiards. An instance of this may be found at Cape Girardeau, Mo., where Major O. H. Ernst has removed a bar in front of the town by works placed several miles above, and on the opposite side of the river.

Amid the unstable conditions thus produced by caving banks it would be impossible to maintain the improved channel obtained by means of the contraction works which I have described, however successful they may be at the start. Hence it is indispensable to hold the banks whose caving would be likely to result in changes in the improved reaches.

This part of the work is, beyond doubt, the most difficult, and to the casual observer, witnessing the rate at which fields and forests are devoured by the river, may well seem impossible. But the measure of the possibility of such an undertaking is not its aggregate vastness. It is an end to be reached by steps, and the practicability of each step severally is the true test of the possibility of the whole. It will be seen on close observation that the Mississippi river tears down its banks as it builds them up—little by little. A caving bank rises straight up from from the water edge, anywhere from ten to forty feet. At its base there is an incessant lapping and chafing, by which it is slowly worn away and undermined. As a consequence it breaks down, piece by piece, and falls into the river, and is there dissolved and carried away. All this is without any violence of attack. The swell of a steamboat breaks against the bank with some force, and occasionally the river puts on a few diminutive white caps under a gale; but for the most part the undulations that play along its margin are ripples rather than waves. There is never anything like the shock of an ocean breaker on the shore. The mischief is done by wavelets, whose action is more like the work of an infinite army of mice, sapping and mining at the foot of the bank, each excavating its teaspoonful per minute. To check this disintegration over a square yard of surface is a light matter.

A woolen blanket laid smoothly against the bank would do it at once. Indeed, the device used for this purpose is next thing to a blanket, a being a mattress—made, however, of brush and poles instead of hair or husk.

This fabric, which holds an important place in many modern engineering works, is woven for use in the Mississippi in webs about one hundred and forty to fifty feet wide, and anywhere from one or two hundred to several thousand feet in length, with slim, flexible willows, twenty to thirty feet long, worked in, top, stem, and branches, for woof, and larger poles, iron rods, or steel wire, for warp. It is made on a boat having a length equal to the width of the mattress, and as it is completed it slides down inclined ways to the water. It can be carried continuously to any length, and in practice is made in such lengths as are best adapted to the bank surface where it is to be used. It is intended that its inner edge shall extend to the foot of the under water slope of the bank, and its outer edge to a point a little below the low water surface. It is sunk and held in place by stone. From the low water margin to the top of the bank the earth is graded to a flat slope. In some places this completes the work. The sunken mattress prevents undermining below the low water line, and the grading down of the overhanging bank stops the undermining above that line. In other, and most cases, the space between the upper edge of the mattress and the line of willow growth is protected by a covering of loose stone. Above that line willows are the most perfect protection possible, and one which nature speedily provides. All this—mattress, grading and stone covering—is embraced in the general term "revetment."

The works which I have thus described comprise all that is done in the channel of the river, and are commonly referred to for distinction as "channel works." They are in the nature of local regulations of the river's flow. In addition to these, there is contemplated in the plan adopted, another regulation, on a larger scale, and more general in effect, viz.: the concentration of all the ordinary discharge of the river, including its ordinary floods, within its channel. The considerations upon which this principle rests are very simple. The river makes the channel; the greatness of the channel depends upon the greatness of the river; the strength of the river is in its water; a waste of its volume is a waste of strength; concentration of its volume is conservation of strength and increase of energy. These observations apply to all ordinary stages of water,— high as well as low, but not to extraordinary or phenomenal floods, which occur at long and irregular intervals. It is doubtful whether it would be advantageous to confine the latter class of floods within the channel, even if no question of cost were involved; it is certain that it would not be wise economy to undertake it for the sake of channel improvement merely. While there is a clear distinction between the ordinary and the extraordinary floods, in their relation to the channel, it is not easy to locate exactly the line which divides them. Upon this subject studies and investigations are in progress, on which, it hoped, more definite conclusions can be based than any yet reached. For the present, all that can be said is, that the ordinary flood is that which occurs with approximate regularity from year to year, and which reaches an elevation not greatly above the normal bank. Within this limit, the high stage and the low stage are the summer and the winter of the river's year ; and to this extent the control of the high stage as well as the low, is a necessary part of any plan of improvement having for its fundamental principle the complete utilization of the natural forces of the river.

The proper order of conducting this part of the work is from the lower reaches upward, and it is desirable that it shall be so executed, if possible, as to close at once an entire alluvial front. At the inception of the work undertaken by the commission, there were found comparatively complete systems of levees along the fronts of the Yazoo and Tensas basins. They were not in all respects such levees as would have been constructed for the purpose of channel improvement, but it was so much cheaper and more expeditious to repair the gaps in them and use them, than to build new ones, that that course was taken. The Yazoo front is now substantially closed, as is also the greater part of the Tensas. The good effects of the concentration of water thus produced, are already apparent. It sent the flood of 1883 from Vicksburg to Red river in undivided volume, and with such velocity and power as to scour out the channel with marked effect. The least depth reported between those two points during the past season was ten and a half feet. The closure of the Tensas front will complete all work of this kind in immediate contemplation. It will be desirable to allow that part of the river directly affected by the work there done, time to adjust itself to the new demands made upon it, before increasing them. The St. Francis front is all that will remain to be closed. There is not at hand there any such system of levees as existed in front of the Yazoo and the Tensas. The work will be to a great extent new, and will have to be constructed either upon such plan as may be adopted with a view to the improvement of the channel alone, (which will not suffice for secure protection against overflow), or else at an expense which the commission does not feel warranted in recommending.

It is proper to observe in this connection, (as upon this point there has been some misapprehension,) that Congress has never authorized the construction of any levees for the protection of lands from overflow. In all the appropriations except the first it has been expressly provided that the money should not be expended for that purpose. The organic act, which I have quoted, mentions the prevention of destructive floods as one of the subjects to be considered, and it has been embraced, to some extent, in the investigations and reports of the commission. But no money has been expended in the construction or repair of any levees except such as were believed to be necessary part of the work of channel improvement.

From the six reaches which I have named, the Plum Point reach and the Lake Providence reach were selected as the first in which the work of improvement should be undertaken. The

former is some sixty miles above Memphis, and the latter
about the same distance above Vicksburg. This choice was
made partly because these two reaches were, all things considered, the worst on the river, and partly because, being
nearly four hundred miles apart, and one of them well toward
the foot of bad navigation, they were, in some respects, typi-
cal localities, and furnished opportunities for thorough tests
and comparisons of means to be employed. It was considered that any device or method which should be found successful at both those places, could be safely employed on any
part of the river.

As must necessarily be the case in any work of such nov-
elty, difficulty, and magnitude, the first year was spent in get-
ting ready to begin. An extensive plant was required, much
of which had to be designed, and all of which had to be contracted and built. Although a large sum was spent for that
purpose before the work began, the supply was inadequate, and
has been largely increased since. Nearly all the channel work
is done from boats, and a great part of it with machinery.
There are floating pile-drivers that drive piles in water twenty
feet deep, and into the ground twenty feet, without a stroke of
the hammer, by means of a hydraulic jet. There are snag-
boats that will jerk a snag out of a bank in less time than a
dentist will extract one from a jaw. There are hydraulic
graders that grade caving banks to a flat slope with water-jets,
at a cost of three and a half cents per cubic yard, —a work
which would cost from twelve to twenty cents if done with
shovel and spade. There is a mattress-boat carrying a steam
loom, which, being fed wire and brush, turns out a continuous
woven mattress one hundred and thirty feet wide and of un-
limited length. There are floating machine and repair shops;
floating boarding-houses, with appliances for feeding and lodg-
ing, all told, nearly two thousand men; and stone, brush, and
coal barges in great number. The entire plant, as now organized, not including snag-boats belonging to the United States,
or chartered tow-boats, embraces 189 barges, 62 pile-drivers,

25 mattress-boats, 39 quarter boats, 5 tow-boats, 4 screen-boats, 3 machine-shop boats, 4 graders, 1 pumping-boat, and 1 steam-tug, making 333 in all, and representing a cost of over a million dollars.

Large as is this outfit, it is none too large, and could be increased in some particulars with advantage. Experience has shown that each integral portion of the work, once undertaken, must be carried by a single assault. To revet part of a caving bank, or half close a chute, and then stop, hazards the safety of all that has been done. It is therefore necessary that there shall be such ample equipment in every department, that prompt advantage can be taken of favorable season, stage, and other conditions, to begin, carry forward, and finish extensive works with the utmost dispatch.

Plum Point reach is twenty miles long, and in some parts nearly two miles wide. It embraces eleven bars, some of them, heretofore, among the worst on the river. It contains five chutes which are to be closed, varying from six hundred to thirty-four hundred feet in width. Its complete improvement will require the revetment of six caving banks, of which the shortest is half a mile, and the longest four miles in length. Permeable dikes have been constructed across four of the chutes to be closed. No work has been done in the fifth, known as Yankee bar chute, because it is hoped that the influence of the works above it will suffice to close it. The effect produced by these structures has exceeded all anticipations. The quantity of earth which has been deposited by means of them is enormous. The deepest fill in any one place is thirty-five vertical feet. In Elmot chute there has been an average fill of six and a half feet, distributed over an area of five hundred acres; in upper Osceola chute an average of five and a half feet, distributed over two hundred and forty acres; and in Bullerton seven feet, distributed over two hundred and fifty acres. While the closure of these chutes is, as yet, only partially complete, it has produced a large concentration of water in the main channel, which has been followed by marked and gratifying results. The bars which formerly obstructed navigation have been cut down from six to ten feet throughout the reach. The last season was one of unusually low water— the lowest within ten years. In other parts of the river five and six feet depths were not uncommon. But here there was a twelve feet channel throughout the season. If every part of the river had been as good as the Plum Point reach, the "J. M. White" and the "Natchez" could have raced from New Orleans to Cairo, in dead low water.

This partial victory over Jupiter Fluvius, (it I may be allowed to create a deity for the occasion), has not been won without loss. It was a campaign against an adversary whose resources, stratagems and methods had to be learned by actual encounter. When the first picket lines of piles were put out to "feel the enemy," it sometimes happened that the enemy felt them and they disappeared. A few strategic points had to be taken and re-taken at heavy cost before they could be finally held. At the head of Elmot chute—the Sevastopol of Plum Point reach, nearly one hundred and fifty thousand dollars worth of work was lost before the river consented to give up its old by-path. This is the heaviest loss that has occurred so far, and is not likely to be repeated elsewhere, although losses, from various inevitable causes, will necessarily occur with greater or less frequency. These permeable dikes, while very easy to describe, nevertheless present many nice questions in their construction which can be settled only by experiment and experience. Thus, as they are to serve only a temporary purpose, it is desirable to put no more money in them than is absolutely necessary: and yet they must be made strong enough to stand unmoved while they are in service. Where they are exposed to active bottom scour, it is necessary to protect them with foot mats, which are brush mattresses, made substantially like those used on the banks, only lighter and narrower, and laid on the river bottom, alongside and among the piles. But where these can be omitted safely it is desirable to avoid the expense of them, as they represent a considerable item of cost. If the dikes are made too open the water flows through them so rapidly that it deposits but little sediment below them ; if they are made too close, they dam up the water, and provoke the river to dig them out. If they are made too low, the floods go over them without sufficient diminution of velocity to cause rapid deposit ; if they are made too high, drift lodges against them, and accumulates in rafts which finally break them down. To hit the golden mean between all these extremes is the desideratum, and it is only by the carpenter's rule of "cut and try" that this can be done. In the interest of economy it is obvious wisdom to begin with the cheapest forms of construction which it is believed will answer the purpose, and advance from those to stronger and costlier devices if it shall prove necessary. The dikes at Elmot chute that were swept away were the first that were put in. They were, as results have shown, too high and too weak, and lower and stronger forms are now used. Although I have spoken of them as lost, they did not exist in vain. Besides the valuable experience which they afforded, they resisted attack long enough to cause large deposits in Elmot chute, and so perished like a soldier on the field, who, before he falls, helps to win the victory which he does not live to see.

When the work was begun, it was regarded as somewhat uncertain whether or not the water in the lower reaches of the river would prove as *rich* as it is in the upper portions—say at St. Louis and thereabout—and capable of yielding as large deposits of sediment. And for that reason the effect of the contraction works at the Lake Providence reach, was looked for with a good deal of anxiety. But all apprehensions on that score have been completely removed by the results, which I will state.

The Lake Providence reach is thirty-five miles long, and in some places nearly two miles wide. It contains eleven bars and nine chutes, in seven of which permeable dikes have been built. Its improvement, as now projected, comprises the revetment of seven caving banks, varying from one and a half to eight miles in length, and making a total of twenty-two and one-half miles. Some of this bank protection may prove to be unnecessary if the work already done, and some yet to do, shall produce the full effect hoped for. In Skipwith chute a fill of thirty-two vertical feet has occurred, and the total fill in that chute measures ten million, three hundred thousand cubic yards. In Stack Island chute a fill of forty-seven vertical feet has been secured since last September. In Baleshed chute five miles and a half of permeable dike have been built, and the deposit produced measures thirty-three million cubic yards. The aggregate deposits in the Lake Providence chutes cover over three thousand acres. The building up of such areas of solid land from particles as minute as a pin-point, carried by flowing water and laid down a speck at a time, is a phenomenon which fairly staggers the imagination.

By means of these works a channel depth of fifteen feet was maintained in Lake Providence reach during the low water of the last season. I saw it stated in one of the river papers not long since that last year, for the first time in her history, the "J. M. White," the largest steamer on the river, made regular trips throughout the season to points above Lake Providence.

I have thus stated, briefly in one sense, but tediously to you, I fear, what is proposed, and what has been done toward the improvement of the lower Mississippi. The question that inevitably follows is, "Will it last?" To this I can only say "I don't know." No one knows. Time alone will tell. Work of this kind is not new. It has been employed with successful results in other parts of the world, but not upon such a scale, and under such circumstances as to furnish reliable precedents. So far as it has gone, the work has fulfilled every expectation of its success. In most respects there is absolute assurance of its continued success. It is certain that permeable dikes can be constructed that will stand, and that they will produce deposits of sediment sufficient to close a chute. It is certain that the concentration of water produced by closing the chutes, and narrowing the channel where it is excessively wide, will scour out the bars to ample depth for navigation. The only thing that remains in any sort of doubt is the practicability of permanently holding the banks. As to that nothing short of the experience of a number of years to come will settle the question. It will not be settled even by repeated failures in particular places. It is a kind of work in which there is wide room for invention and improvement. When I see how much better the devices and methods now employed are than those of only three years ago, I can not doubt that the next three years will show still further advances in the same direction. As to the final result there is not much value in the opinion of any man, and least of all in mine. But there is one element of the problem which I think important, and will mention. I believe that the preservation of the banks depends largely on the maintenance of certain favoring natural conditions in the river, which I will endeavor to describe.

Between Cairo and the gulf there is a fall of three hundred and twenty-two feet. To a river as great as the Mississippi the journey down such a declivity is like the descent of a very fat man down a very steep hill. To go straight down is impossible, without going headlong. So the river lays out its path in curves, and thus diminishes its slope by increasing its length, exactly as an engineer, in laying out a wagon road, or a railway track, down a mountain side, reduces his grades by adopting a circuitous route. By this means the river seeks to reduce its own velocity to a rate which its banks can bear without destruction. It follows that the crookedness of its channel is no accident, or misfortune, but a piece of Nature's own wise engineering; and that the hope once expressed by a high official, that the first work of the commission would be to take some of the "kinks" out of the river, was wide the mark. The most perfect condition of the river possible is that in which there is the most perfect equilibrium possible between the velocity of its current and the strength of its banks. It is

in search of this equilibrium that it increases its length and
flattens its slope by enlarging its bends. But the enlargement
of the bends tends to narrow the necks of land between them,
and so, in course of time, to cut them off. And the result of
such a cut-off is to undo all the equalizing work of years before,
and introduce chaos and change through a series of years following. Take, for example, a bend twenty miles in length as
the current flows, and with a fall of three inches per mile.
When the neck of land between the extremities of the bend
gives way, there is introduced at that point a sudden fall equal
to the entire former fall around the bend, which would be, in
the case supposed, five feet. The increased velocity produced
by such a change is irresistible, and the banks for miles above
and below the cut-off melt away like ash-heaps. If there happens to be another narrow neck not far below, it is certain to
give way shortly; and thus the river runs riot, until its violence works its own cure by re-creating the bends, and so
restoring its normal length and velocity. We have thus produced alternate periods of stability and of change, each lasting
through a number of years, and each tending to produce the
other. During a long period of stability the river makes for
itself hundreds of miles of perfect channel, down which it flows
through curves of ample sweep, and between sloping banks
that show little change from year to year.

The present is a period of comparative stability. No great
cut-off has occurred since that at Vicksburg, in 1876. And
you will find in the river to-day many long reaches of model
channel. The gist of the present plan is to copy the models
which nature thus offers. That this can be done with approximate fidelity is certain, and I see no reason why the improved
channel, once secured, may not be permanently preserved,
without extravagant cost, as long as the conditions of general
stability continue. But if the river be allowed to break
through these, even to the extent of a single cut-off, it will be
like a runaway horse—there is no telling where it will stop.
I do not mean by this that such a catastrophe would neces-

sarily destroy improvements then completed, or render other improvements impossible ; but it would introduce such grave and additional difficulties into the problem that its solution would become a matter of renewed doubt and experiment. And in order to prevent any such lapse into evil ways on the part of the river, there will be required careful watchfulness, and prompt measures of prevention when danger threatens. With these favoring conditions maintained, I believe that the work of bank protection, which is the key of the whole scheme, can be successfully accomplished and permanently held.

I have taxed your patience to such a degree in description of the works in progress on the lower river, that I am compelled to omit any extended reference to those above Cairo. I can only say that a few miles below your own city, on Horsetail bar, are channel works precisely similar to those at Plum Point and Lake Providence, which have been in progress for several years, under the charge of Major O. H. Ernst, of the Engineers, and which have proven quite as successful as those below.

Above the mouth of the Illinois river are other works, designed also to deepen and improve the channel, but entirely different in character from those which I have described, which are being successfully carried on under the able direction of Major Mackenzie, of the Engineers. But of either of these I can not speak now at length.

I desire to add, before closing, a word of deserved tribute to the accomplished officers of the Engineer Corps who are in charge of the works on the lower river. If those works succeed, it is to them that the country will owe most thanks for it. It is upon their invention, resources, courage, prudence and executive ability that everything depends. To the difficulties and responsibilities of the work, are added the deadly dangers of fatigue and exposure in a malarial climate. An active military campaign is a less perilous undertaking than a summer on the improvement works of the lower

Mississippi to an unacclimated white man. Brave men who thus take their lives in hand at the call of duty, deserve not only the thanks of their countrymen, but substantial recognition by Congress and the government.

OUTLETS.

FROM THE NORTH AMERICAN REVIEW, MARCH, 1883.

The Mississippi River Commission was created by Act of Congress, approved June 28, 1879. It consists of seven members, appointed by the President, of whom three are required to be from the Engineer Corps of the Army, one from the Coast and Geodetic Survey, and three from civil life, of whom two shall be civil engineers. It is provided in the act that the commission shall—

Take into consideration and mature such plan or plans and estimates as will correct, permanently locate, and deepen the channel and protect the banks of the Mississippi River; improve and give safety and ease to the navigation thereof, prevent destructive floods, and promote and facilitate commerce, trade, and the postal service.

The commission was duly organized, and, after consideration of the subject, reported a plan of improvement, which has been adopted by Congress, and for the execution of which an appropriation of $1,000,000 was made by Act of March 3, 1881, and another of $4,123,000 by Act of August 2, 1882, all to be expended below Cairo. Under these appropriations the work is now in progress, its execution being in the hands of officers of the Engineer Corps detailed for that purpose by the Chief of Engineers. Its completion, according to the plans proposed, will require a number of years, and further large appropriations. There is added, therefore, to the interest which belongs to the subject as a great engineering problem, that which attaches to every object of public expenditure.

It is the purpose of this article to set forth briefly the general plan proposed by the commission, and the reasons upon which it rests. In order to a clear apprehension of the questions involved, a short description of the river in its unimproved condition will be found useful.

At the city of Cairo, upon the southern extremity of the State of Illinois, are gathered together the waters of five great rivers, viz.: the Missouri, the Upper Mississippi, the Ohio, the Cumberland, and the Tennessee. Between that point and the Gulf of Mexico, lies the Mississippi River proper, 1,097 miles in length as it flows. Its course is through an alluvial plain, six hundred miles long and from twenty-five to eighty miles wide. In this basin is embraced an area of 41,000 square miles, of which 32,000 square miles are liable to overflow. Borings made at eighty three places between Cairo and Vicksburg show one hundred and thirty-one feet mean depth of alluvial soil. From Cairo to the mouth of the Red, the width of the river between banks varies from 1,900 to 13,800 feet, the mean being 4,400 feet. Below the Red the width rarely exceeds 3,500, the mean being 3,350. Between Cairo and Memphis its least depth at low water is five feet; between Memphis and Red River, six feet; and between Red River and New Orleans, fifteen feet. The variation in its discharge is enormous, passing from 100,000 cubic feet per second at low water to 1,800,000 at the highest flood. The range between high and low water mark at Cairo is fifty two feet; at Memphis, thirty-five feet; at Vicksburg, fifty-two feet; and at New Orleans, fourteen feet. In its greatest floods its water surface stretches from hill to hill, across the entire valley; at extreme low water, it flows between banks from thirty to forty feet high. The depth of its inundation bears no comparison with its area, being, on an average, less than three feet over the arable lands. In the swamps it is much more. Its flood elevation at Cairo is three hundred and twenty-two feet above the sea. Its fall from Cairo to Memphis is about six inches to the mile. Thence to the gulf its fall steadily diminishes, being about one and a half inches per mile at New Orleans. It is one of the muddiest rivers in the world. The greater portion of the sediment received by it at

Cairo comes from the Missouri, but this supply is constantly reinforced by the caving of its own banks, which are washed into the river at an estimated rate of 5,000 acres per annum.

All plans for the improvement of the Mississippi that have been prominently discussed rest upon one of two theories : one, that the remedy for the evils existing consists, essentially, in the concentration of the water of the river and the equalization of its flow ; the other, that it consists in the subdivision and diffusion of its volume. The former theory is the one held by the commission and adopted by Congress, though the other has advocates, whose views continue to be urged in Congress and through the press.

There are numerous opportunities to let out of the channel of the Mississippi large portions of its water. The Atchafalaya, which receives its water from the Red River, at a point only six miles distant from the junction of that river with the Mississippi, is there several feet lower than the Mississippi. At the present time the water of the Red rarely reaches the Mississippi at all, but, for the most part, flows down the Atchafalaya, augmented by a large flow from the Mississippi. It is only when the Red is high and the Mississippi low, that there is any flow from the former to the latter. The difference of level between the Mississippi and the Atchafalaya increases as they descend, so that at Plaquemine the difference is twenty-two feet, and the distance betwen them eleven miles. On the east bank, at Bonnet Carre, the difference of level between the river and Lake Ponchartrain is twenty feet, and the distance between them five miles. At Lake Borgne the difference of level is fourteen feet and the distance six miles. So that it is quite possible to make outlets by which the flood-water, or, for that matter, all the water of the Mississippi, could find its way to the gulf by shorter lines and lower levels than those of the present river. And when men stand appalled at the sight of its devastating floods, the suggestion of quick relief by outlets seems at first sight so practicable and reasonable that it is not strange that it should find favor in many minds.

The reasons which lie against this theory require some thought for their clear apprehension, but rest, as is believed, on well ascertained laws.

The three most difficult factors in the problem are, the wide variation in the volume of the river's discharge, the quantity of solid matter transported by its current, and the softness of its banks. If any one of these three elements were absent, the questions presented would be comparatively simple.

To contain the river at its flood requires a great channel. Its banks are so friable that its constant tendency is to make itself room by tearing them down. When the flood subsides the material of which they were composed is found scattered over the broad channel in obstructing bars and shoals. Over and among these the low-water river has to make its way by such tortuous and changing path as it can find or make for itself. It is then that navigation becomes difficult and dangerous. There is water enough in the river at its lowest stage to furnish ample depth for navigation, if it were confined in a channel of suitable width; and it would make and maintain such a channel for itself, if it were not for the interference of the floods.

The problem of the river's improvment comprehends, therefore, in its broadest sense, these two requisites— a high-water channel capacious enough to contain its floods, and a low-water channel narrow enough to afford the depth necessary for navigation. And the more nearly identical in location these can be made, the more permanent and perfect will be the improvement attained.

In the consideration of any plan for the accomplishment of these ends, it is to be remembered that there are very rigid limits to the possibilities of engineering methods applicable to the case. To build upon a foundation of bottomless alluvium any break-water or training-wall of stone or timber, that shall withstand the floods that pour down from the north like an ocean let loose, is impossible. To dig and keep open a channel for a river that flings down in its own pathway a sand bar a mile square as though it were a handful of ashes, is equally impossible. Hence, if at any point a deeper channel is needed, the river must be compelled to dig it; if a new bank is needed, the river must be coaxed to build it. Its own Titanic hands are the only instruments equal to either task.

If any one will set a tumblerful of the coffee-colored water of the Mississippi where it will remain undisturbed for twenty-four hours, he will find, at the end of that time, a teaspoonful of mud in the bottom of the tumbler, while the water will be comparatively clear. If he had kept the water in motion all the time he would have found it as turbid as when he took it from the river, and no deposit at the bottom. In this tiny experiment is illustrated the most important law of the Mississippi River's life, viz.: that the power of water to sustain and transport sediment depends upon its motion. The exact relation between the velocity of moving water and its silt-carrying power is not ascertained. It varies with the size and specific gravity of the particles. But enough is known to warrant the general statement that every diminution of the velocity of a running stream diminishes its silt-transporting capacity. It is not necessary, in order to produce this result, that there shall be a cessation of motion in the water; a diminution of its rate is sufficient.

The operation of this law is universal and invariable, on the largest scale and on the smallest. The miniature torrent that sweeps down the plowed furrow in a hill-side field scours its bed clean as long as it maintains its headlong velocity. But when it slackens its course at the foot of the slope, it throws down its load of sand and loam in an instant. The delta which forms at the mouth of every sediment-bearing river is the same phenomenon on a larger scale.

Upon the Mississippi River the traveler is never for a moment out of sight of visible evidence of the operation of this law. The following examples will be familiar to any one who has been upon it.

In the outer curve of every bend, where the current is swift and strong, the channel is deep and clean. On the inner side of the return curve there is slack water and a bar. Wherever the channel is narrow and deep, there is a high velocity and no deposit of sediment. Where it is excessively broad and shallow, bars accummulate rapidly.

At a bank full stage the river has a rapid current and is heavily loaded with sediment. At the overflow stage the water escaping laterally over the banks is suddenly checked in its velocity, and immediately begins to drop its load, leaving a diminishing deposit as it recedes. To this layer the next flood adds another, each being thickest at the margin next the river, where the escaping water experiences the first diminution of its velocity. In this way the river builds up its own banks by overflow; and in consequence of this method of building them they are highest nearest the river, the receding declination sometimes reaching twelve feet in a mile, and being rarely less than five.

Following the course of great overflows through the forests adjacent to the river, the observer will find on the farther side of trees, logs, and other obstructions, sand reefs and areas of deposit marking every place where the advancing water was checked in its velocity.

It occasionally happens that the river cuts off a long bend by a short channel across its neck, leaving a horseshoe-shaped section of the old channel unused. At the open ends of this abandoned channel the water in it mingles with the current flowing past, and so has a gentle inward and outward flow as the river rises and falls. The consequence is a deposit of sediment at the entrances of the abandoned channel, by which they are ultimately filled up and cut off entirely from the new channel, forming deep, clear, crescent-shaped lakes. There are many such lakes in the valley, some of them now several miles from the river. Such a cut-off occurred at a bend opposite Vicksburg in 1876, leaving the city upon one arm of the abandoned bend. The lower end of that arm is already filled up to the height of twenty-five feet above low water, and fifty feet above the old bottom, leaving the city's wharves and elevators a mile and a half inland at ordinary and low stages.

By shiftings of the channel, the formation of islands, and other causes, the subsidiary channels, called chutes, are formed in large number. If a swift current set through a chute, it enlarges ; if a sluggish current flow through it, it fills with sediment. Sloughs and outlets leading out of the river into the swamps, in which the free flow of water is obstructed by willows, are often permanently closed in the same manner.

As the river elongates its bends by caving off the outer bank, there is commonly formed a sloping bar on the inner bank, which advances as the outer bank recedes. As fast as this bar rises above ordinary low water, it is covered by a growth of willows. At high stages, the water flowing over the bar is obstructed by this growth, and successive deposits of sediment are thus caused, which ultimately build the bar up to the full height of the adjacent banks. By this process the river shifts its channel, tearing down one bank and building up the other as it goes.

Some of the methods of channel improvement now in use have been copied from the processes of nature just described. When it is sought to narrow an excessively wide channel, permeable screens, made of piles and interwoven brush or poles, are set on the bar where it is desired to form new banks, at intervals of a thousand feet or less. The water, in flowing through these screens, loses so much of its velocity that it drops its sediment very rapidly after passing them. The effect produced by such structures is sometimes quite remarkable. In favorable localities a fill of forty feet in depth has resulted in a single season. At Horsetail Bar, below St. Louis, may be seen an area of more than a thousand acres of land, which has been built up from the river-bed to an average depth of twenty-five feet by the means just described. A mere line of piles, eight feet apart, will often produce a heavy deposit below them.

These numerous examples have been cited in order to illustrate and enforce the proposition stated at the outset ; that the greatest law of the river's life is that it shall be forever laden with a burden which slips from its grasp the instant it loiters by the way. The whole valley is itself the result and the proof of the existence and the operation of this law. There is not a shoveltul of earth in all its square miles that has not been dissolved in water, and carried by water to the point where its journey ended for want of velocity to carry it farther. Every grain of sand, every drop of water, every inch of movement, every low stage, every high stage, every flood, is equally obedient to the same great law. The engineer who has learned its meaning well has taken the first step toward a successful solution of the problem of the river's improvement. He who ignores or defies it puts himself in the pathway of forces as irresistible in their operation as the march of a glacier.

This brings us to the practical question. Here are so many cubic miles of water per annum to be conducted to the sea. It is desired to do it in such manner as to afford the best possible low-water navigation, and the least possible high-water inundation. Shall it be confined in its course to one channel, or shall it be subdivided or allowed to subdivide itself into several ?

The excavation of a river channel is work. The transportation of sediment is work. The accomplishment of either involves the expenditure of energy. So that it is but another statement of the same question to say : How will a given quantity of water perform most work—in one concentrated volume, or in subdivisions?

To this inquiry the experience of every person furnishes a ready and true answer. A gentle rain, falling on the earth's surface, leaves its lightest vegetable mold undisturbed. The same quanty of water, descending in a waterspout, tears away its solid hills. The water which trickles over a field through thousands of infinitesimal and broken channels, without producing the least abrasion of its surface, would, if concentrated in one volume on the same surface, plow it deep and wide. There is nothing else in nature of which it is so literally and familiarly true that "in union there is strength," as of water. Subdivided finely enough, it is the morning mist; concentrated largely enough, it is nature's master mechanic, the continent-builder of the world.

Taking its whole life together, there is, in the phenomena of the Missisippi River, as elsewhere, a perfect correlation of forces. It does all the work it can all the time. It excavates its bed as deep and wide as it can. It carries out of its channel as much of the sediment mixed with its water as it can. When it drops from its broad shoulders a hundred thousand cubic yards of sand on one bar, as it often does, it is because it can carry it no farther. It never drops a spoonful except for the same reason.

All the conditions of the river are the result of its own forces. It has no antecedent banks, bars, width or depth ; all these are its own creation. It made yesterday the things that make it to-day ; it is making to-day the things that will make it to-morrow. Its present inadequacy to meet the wants of men is the result of its inadequate work in the past. It overflows its banks because its channel is not capacious enough to contain its flood. To make its channel more capacious requires more work. At low water it stumbles over bars which it lacks strength to displace. To remove them requires more work. It makes its shoal places shoaler by the deposit of sediment which it wants energy to carry farther. More work would do it. So that if the river of the future is to subserve the interests of mankind better than the river of the present, the river of to-day must be induced to do more and better work. This is to be accomplished by the conservation, concentration, and wise direction of all its energies. That this means the conservation, concentration, and wise direction of its *volume* seems too obvious to need repetition.

Depletion, or subdivision, is a step in exactly the wrong

direction. It is a change toward weakness ; not toward strength. An outlet may serve to lower a flood for the time being, but the result is a temporary advantage gained at enormous future cost. The diminution of volume produced by the outlet means diminution of energy. It means a smaller, weaker river from that point to the sea. And that means a river less able to remove bars, less able to excavate a channel, less able to carry sediment, less able to contain a flood.

It is in the nature of things that each portion of the river shall, in its turn, bear the burden of the complications above it. The bars that obstruct it came down from above. Hence, there is the clearest necessity that it should, as in the order of nature it does, augment its strength as it descends. An outlet reverses this order of nature and of reason. It diminishes the energy of the river below, without lightening, in any like degree, the burdens cast upon it by the river above.

It is not possible, without accurate and expensive observations and measurements, to trace all the injurious effects of an outlet upon the river below. But enough is visible to common observation to show the unvarying operation of the laws stated. At its mouth the Mississippi has tried the outlet system of its own accord, by subdividing into four distinct channels. From New Orleans down to the widening of the channel, preparatory to its subdivision, it has nowhere less than a hundred feet of depth. In its four subordinate channels the depth rarely exceeds fifty feet ; and at the mouths of all, except the one improved by the jetties, it is about sixteen feet. Suppose the same subdivision had taken place two or three hundred miles higher up, would not like results have followed in the channels below ?

Outlets in the form of great crevasses have frequently occurred. They are always followed by increased deposits in the bed below them.

Channels conveying unfiltered Mississippi water invariably contract their dimensions to the smallest space that will contain the water flowing through them. The law governing chutes

has been stated already;—a swift current keeps them open;
a sluggish current fills them up with sediment. When an
island appears in the center of the river, it is rare that a good
channel is maintained on each side of it. Something will
occur to disturb the equilibrum between the two; one will begin
to rob the other of water; whereupon the other will begin
to fill with sediment,—a process which increases in rapidity as
the disproportion of flow grows greater.

At the mouth of the Red River is a remarkable illustration
of the same law. The Red formerly entered the Mississippi
at the apex of a bend. In 1831 the bend was cut off. For a
time the Red used the upper arm of the bend as its channel,
during which time it rapidly contracted to the dimensions suitable for the conveyance of the water of the Red River alone;
while the lower arm of the bend closed up entirely. Afterward
the Red abandoned the upper arm of the bend, and cut a
channel just large enough for its own flow through the lower
one; whereupon the upper one filled up. Later, the enlargement of the lower Atchafalaya, whose head is in the apex of
the old bend, near the original mouth of the Red, produced an
active outflow from the Mississippi, which has been already
described, and, in consequence, the channel is now enlarging.
So that, in the space of six miles, between the Mississippi and
the head of the Atchafalaya, there have been, within fifty years
past, first, a Mississippi channel 3,500 feet wide, and probably
sixty feet deep; then a dry bar; then a Red River channel
three hundred feet wide and ten feet deep; and now a rapidly
growing outlet.

The use of the word "unfiltered" in the general statement
above is material, and marks an important distinction. The
statement is not true of a channel conveying clear water. The
Yazoo River is one of this class. There was formerly, at
Yazoo Pass, nearly opposite Helena, an outlet which diverted
a large volume from the Mississippi into the Yazoo, which
that river returned to the Mississippi at Vicksburg. By this
means the channel of the Yazoo was excavated deep and wide.

The pass was closed a number of years ago. Since then the chief water-supply of the Yazoo has come from the swamp-drains, which discharge clear water, and from Mississippi overflows, which are thoroughly filtered by the woods and swamps through which they travel before reaching it. So that we have to-day in the Yazoo a clear-water stream, flowing with slow velocity through a capacious channel which does not perceptibly decrease in size. No such result ever occurs in the case of water charged with sediment.

Nature has made the channel of the Mississippi of increased capacity for discharge as it descends. The permanent diversion of a substantial portion of its water by outlets will reverse that order, and shrink the channel below them to the size required by the diminished river. This shrinkage will take place first by decrease of depth, as the depositing sediment falls to the bottom, and thus the interests of navigation will be the first to suffer. But the mischief will not stop there. When the river and the outlets shall have adjusted themselves to the new conditions created, they will, all together, be less able to discharge a great flood than the unimpaired river was alone; and there will be no place for it to find vent except over the shallow rim of the shrunken channel.

It is not within the purpose of this article to describe in detail the methods by which it is proposed to execute the general plan of improvement recommended by the Mississippi River Commission. Suffice it to say that the retention of the river's water in one undivided volume is the cardinal principle of the plan; and that it is proposed to seek this end by such means as will introduce the fewest artificial conditions into the river's life, and apply most economically and effectually its its own forces to the work of improving its own channel. These consist chiefly in the closing of chutes and outlets; the contraction of the channel in places where it is excessively wide, by the creation of new banks from deposited sediment; and the revetment of banks where caving is exceptionally rapid and injurious.

LEVEES.

FROM THE NORTH AMERICAN REVIEW, MARCH, 1884.

The building of the jetties has transformed New Orleans into a great sea-port. Fifteen lines of steamers are now employed in her foreign trade. For the year ending June 30, 1883, she was next to New York in value of exports, and ranked third in total foreign commerce; the amount of the latter being $104,704,076. Toward this gate-way of the outer world the Mississippi, with its two thousand miles of main river and ten thousand miles of navigable tributaries, is the natural internal highway. The five feet low-water channel over its bars, which, like the canals of a generation ago, sufficed to meet the wants of commerce in years past, is wholly inadequate for present needs, much more for those of the near future. Recognizing these facts, the United States Government has undertaken to deepen and improve the channel of the Mississippi River. For the accomplishment of that end a plan has been adopted, and is now in course of execution. The salient points of that plan may be stated as follows:

To utilize the scouring power of the river for the purpose of cutting away the bars that obstruct navigation; to apply the energy of the river to this work by narrowing the channel over the bars, and thus concentrating its current upon them, obstructing bars being uniformly coincident with excessive width in the present river bed; to prevent the re-formation of bars by protecting the caving banks above them, from which most of their constituent material is taken; to preserve the energy of the river, unimpaired by outlets or subdivisions of its present volume. In a former number of the REVIEW (March, 1883,) were presented some considerations in support of the theory of concentration as opposed to that of diffusion by outlets as a means of improving the channel of the river. These need not be repeated here.

Assuming it to be sufficiently established for the present purpose that it is necessary for the preservation, and much more for an increase, of the river's present low-water depth that at all ordinary stages it shall flow in one undivided channel of as uniform width as is practicable, there remains this further and important question, viz.: Is it also in accordance with sound principles of engineering, and will it be in like manner conducive to the improvement of the river, to confine its flood volume in the same channel by artificial additions to its natural banks?

In the study of this, as of all other questions relating to the Mississippi, the river itself is the best teacher. It is, and must always remain, a self-made river. If we can discover the means by which its channel has been made as good as it is, we shall have the surest indication of the means by which it may be made better. It is an obvious proposition that these means are all comprised in scour at the bottom and bank building at the sides. It is also obvious that some extent of bank building must precede any considerable excavation by scour. A thin, unconfined sheet of water has little or no scouring power. Bank building takes place by the deposit of sediment in time of overflow, each flood adding its contribution to the pre-existing bank. It is impossible, however, for water to carry a deposit of sediment quite to the elevation of its own surface. So that a flood of given height can not build banks high enough to confine a succeeding flood of equal or greater height; but it may carry them high enough to confine succeeding floods of less height. As matter of fact, while the Mississippi River is constantly fluctuating in its stage, comparatively few of the rises which occur in a year, and rarely more than one, go over the natural bank. For the most part, the stream flows, rises, and falls between banks built for it by ·past floods. These, we will assume, the river has carried to the full height of its unaided arm's length. It is proposed now to make an artificial addition to them in the form of levees. This will do for the greater floods exactly what the greater floods have already done for the lesser,—confine them within a defined channel. Such an addition to the natural bank is plainly a mere continuation of the very process of channel construction by which the present river bed has been made. It is but the finishing of the river's own unfinished work. And if it be a fact that the present magnificent channel, scarcely second to any in the world for navigation, has been created solely by the energy of the water flowing in it, will not an increase of that energy by increase of volume and depth necessarily increase the river's capacity for work, and so result in a deeper and better channel?

There is no doubt that the ability of the Mississippi River to maintain its normal bank height has been greatly diminished by artificial causes. Before the advent of civilized man in its upper valley, every forest, swamp, and grass-covered prairie helped to hold back the rain-fall. The effect of clearing, draining, and cultivation has been to send the surplus water of that vast region into the lower river in sudden, short-lived, enormous floods. Furthermore, in a state of nature, the banks of the lower river were everywhere covered with a dense mass of vegetation, which formed a perfect filter for separating the sediment from the overflowing water, and also furnished great protection against caving. Now they are occupied in large part by cleared fields, over which the flood water passes with comparatively little loss of sediment, and which wash into the river easily and rapidly. So that it may be said with truth that the artificial addition of a few feet to the present natural bank is scarcely more than the river itself would accomplish by natural agencies but for the interference of man. There is evidence that the Mississippi had once a narrower channel and higher banks than at present. As a rule, the ancient, crescent-shaped lakes in the valley, which, it is certain, were formerly parts of the river bed, have banks higher than those of the present river, with intervening width considerably less.

There is another consideration of different, but not less important, character. The fluid which fills the channel of the

Mississippi is not, as we are apt to assume, water merely, but a mixture of water and soil,—a fact which can not be left out of sight for a moment in studying the phenomena of the river. From this flowing mixture, the soil tends constantly to separate. Every diminution of its velocity results in a deposit of solid matter at the bottom. Unrestrained overflow tends to produce diminished and irregular velocity in the main channel, and so to fill it up with sediment.

The grand alluvial basin of the lower Mississippi lies in four natural subdivisions, known respectively as the St. Francis, the Yazoo, the Tensas, and the Atchafalaya basins, or fronts. The general surface elevation of each of these basins is lower than that of the immediate banks of the river. The water which escapes across the upper portion of the St. Francis front during an overflowing flood, fills up that basin and flows downward through it until it meets the high lands which touch the river at Helena, where it is forced back into the river. In like manner, the water which escapes across the Yazoo front is forced into the river again by the bluffs at Vicksburg. There result, in consequence, first, a division of the river's volume at the head of each basin, by which its velocity and energy are diminished ; and second, an enormous accumulation of water at the foot of each basin, by which its flood level is raised .to an abnormal height.

The great floods of 1882 and 1883 presented in this respect a remarkable contrast. That of '82 had free access into the Yazoo basin through numerous gaps in the levees. Prior to the flood of '83, these were repaired so far as to exclude the latter flood almost entirely. During the flood of '82, the maximum stage at Cairo was 51.87 feet above low water ; at Memphis, 35.15 ; at Vicksburg, 48.75. During the flood of '83, the maximum at Cairo was 51.90 ; at Memphis, 35.11 ; at Vicksburg, 43.80. Thus, while the two floods reached almost exactly the same height at Cairo and Memphis, the second fell off 4.95 feet at Vicksburg. The difference is very significant. A reduction of five feet in Mississippi flood level means a great deal. At the maximum stage of '82, the river was thirty miles wide at Vicksburg : at that of '83, it was almost within its banks. The former flood exhibits the action of a slowly moving lake ; the latter that of a running river. One flowed steadily toward the sea ; the other loitered about over eight thousand square miles of land. After passing Vicksburg, the flood of '83 remained substantially within banks to the Red River. The season following was one of unusually low water. In the upper parts of the river, where the overflow had been greatest, many bars showed only six feet of depth, and some only five. But from Vicksburg down there was abundant and unusual depth throughout the season, no bars showing less than ten feet. The scouring force of this one partially confined flood seems to have produced a marked improvement through one hundred and sixty-eight miles of channel.

The unrestrained overflow of flood-water is also accompanied by constantly recurring local variations of velocity and direction in the main channel. Some parts of the bank are lower than others ; some cleared smooth, others covered with timber ; some furnish open pathways to capacious reservoirs or bayous, others do not. So that the quantity of water escaping from one part of the river may be very great ; from another part, a few miles below, very little. These irregular discharges produce corresponding fluctuations in the velocity and direction of the current, and consequent retardation of flow and deposits of sediment.

An overflow through a series of crevasses located not far distant from each other is substantially like an overflow across the natural bank. The chief difference is that in the former case the sections of discharge are more sharply defined than in the latter, where there is likely to be a thin sheet running over a considerable portion of the entire front, with large discharges at bayous or depressions in the surface. During the flood of '82, a group of four crevasses occurred on the Yazoo front within a space of eighty miles, the upper one being at

Malone's Landing, sixty miles below Memphis, and the others at Riverton, Bolivar, and Mound Place, respectively. The river along this front had been carefully surveyed during the months of January and February of that year, and its depth and cross section at all those points, very shortly prior to the outflow, were accurately known. In October following,—the outflow having occurred in the meantime,—a re-survey was made of the river opposite and several miles below each of these crevasses, for the purpose of ascertaining what change, if any, had been produced by them. The results showed a marked filling up of the bed in every case. At Malone's Landing, a small crevasse, the fill amounted to four per cent. of the entire channel space ; at Riverton, to fourteen ; at Bolivar, eleven ; at Mound Place, twenty-four : being an average of thirteen per cent. These overflows, being circumscribed in extent and large in amount, produced correspondingly great shoalings of the water-way within like short spaces. If the same amount of overflow had been distributed over a longer bank front, it is probable that the resulting impairment of the channel would not have been so great at any one place, or so easy to ascertain and measure ; but that the tendency and consequence of it would have been the same in kind, seems a very obvious inference.

During the years 1881 and 1882, systematic observations were conducted by the Government at several stations on the Mississippi, to determine its depth, cross section or vertical water area, mean velocity, and discharge, besides some other matters not material here. In these observations may be found some striking illustrations of the tendency of an alluvial stream to obstruct its own path during overflow. At Clayton, Iowa, where general overflow begins at the fourteen feet stage, observations taken during the flood of October, 1881, showed that at that stage the velocity of the current, which up to that time had increased as the water rose, suddenly ceased to increase, and remained substantially unchanged until the rise reached its maximum of eighteen feet, seventeen days later.

That is to say, the river rose four feet above its banks without any increase of velocity in its current.

Like observations taken at Grafton, Ill., during the flood of April and May of the same year, showed that as the river rose above its ordinary stage, the velocity of its current and the amount of water discharged increased in the usual accelerating ratio until the stage of general overflow was reached. At that point the velocity and discharge ceased to increase, and, during the last two feet of rise, both actually diminished. To be exact, on April 25th, the stage was 32.17 ft., cross section 67,545 sq. ft., mean velocity 4,594 ft. per sec., discharge 310,309 cu. ft. per sec.; while on May 6th the stage was 34.16, cross section 73,695, velocity 3,859, and discharge 284,405. That is, the river ran with nine inches per second less velocity, and discharged nearly twenty six thousand cubic feet per second less water at its highest stage than when two feet lower.

At Hay's Landing, Miss., the gauge reading March 20, 1882, was 38.58, cross section 172,105, mean velocity 5.44, discharge 936,900. Ten days afterward, when the river had passed from general overflow to bank-full stage, the gauge reading was 34.14, cross section 167,396, mean velocity 6.26, discharge 1,049,000. That is, a fall of four and a half feet from the maximum, which brought the river within its banks, increased its velocity eight-tenths of a foot, and its discharge a hundred and twelve thousand cubic feet, per second.

In April, 1881, an unusual flood occurred in the Missouri. It originated above Sioux City, and was not augmented by any floods from its tributaries, below. For a distance of five hundred miles it covered the valley from bluff to bluff. There was nothing to retard its progress, except such obstruction as it created itself. Nevertheless, its velocity so slackened as it rose above its banks, and its rise so increased as its velocity slackened, that it reached a height at St. Charles three feet above its relative height at Sioux City; whereas, the normal course of a flood is to diminish in height above the low water plane as it flows downward. It was observed, also, that the amount of water discharged was less than that which the river was accustomed to discharge at a height seven feet below that of the flood, and within the banks.

It is to be remembered, of course, that in the production of such phenomena as these many forces may co-operate, and they should not be hastily ascribed to a single cause. But it is obvious that in each of these cases there was a choke of some kind in the river. There was no visible obstruction in any of them to create it. It was coincident with general overflow, and did not appear at any other stage. The inference from these circumstances alone, that it was in some way caused by the overflow, is by no means illogical. But there are better grounds for that conclusion than mere coincidence.

A stream of water loaded to its full carrying capacity with sediment, is exceedingly sensitive to change. The particles of sediment swim by means of their friction. Two particles that can barely swim separately will sink if brought in contact, because the contact reduces their aggregate frictional surface. In falling, they will carry down myriads of other particles that can barely swim. So that the least halt in the great procession of particles precipitates part of its constituent membership to the bottom. There they create an obstruction which prolongs the halt; the prolonged halt increases the obstruction, and so on, each condition reacting upon the other. The result is decreased velocity and increased rise in the stream. Just how slight a cause may start this train of causes, it is impossible to tell.

The Mississippi River at Cairo knows nothing of the Gulf of Mexico. It does not flow from love of motion, but in search of rest. Its condition of rest is levelness of surface. Confined in a narrow, descending channel, it can find no rest until it dies in the ocean. But when it overtops its banks there is comparative rest nearer at hand. It becomes a river flowing through a lake. Its buried channel no longer compels it to seek its level in one direction only. It may seek it in any direction and over thousands of square miles of surface. Moreover, the multiplied curves of the buried channel often lead in directions inconsistent with the general slope of the valley. And so, when the valley is turned into a lake, the slope of the lake surface will sometimes harmonize with, and sometimes contradict, the slope which the river had when within its banks. Amid these complicated conditions, the water pursues its unvarying purpose to seek its level on all sides, and so flows in whatever direction, and with whatever speed, tend most to that end. These considerations alone will go far to account for the piling up of a flood by wide-spread overflow. Thicken the water with sediment, and such a result ceases to be surprising.

Levees have not been constructed heretofore for the purpose of channel improvement. But they have been in use from time immemorial, and in many parts of the world, for protection against overflow, and have in many instances produced an unintended deepening of the channels between them.

Red River, from Shreveport to its mouth, flows by a crooked channel through an alluvial basin like that of the Mississippi, and is a stream of like behavior with the main river. A few years before the war its levees were made complete and continuous on both sides for a distance of two hundred miles above Alexandria. Their effect in deepening the channel was so marked and immediate that in a few years such floods as had formerly overspread the valley for miles, found room for discharge within the banks, and rarely reached the levees at all. Elsewhere, the shallow channel remained and the river overflowed as before.

The Lafourche is a bayou heading in the Mississippi at Donaldsonville, seventy-seven miles above New Orleans, and flowing thence through the Atchafalaya basin to the Gulf. Its upper portion, for a distance of some sixty-five miles, has been leveed for sixty years. In its lower portion, overflow is unrestrained. Its upper portion has maintained its depth unimpaired. In its lower portion the deposit of sediment has so raised its bed and obstructed its discharge that it has become necessary to build the levees, at and near their lower termini, higher and higher in order to resist the floods, until now they extend eight feet above their original height; while those above, where the stream has been kept within its channel, remain as they were fifty years ago.

Abroad, the Po, the Rhine, the Seine, and the Thames may be cited as examples of rivers whose channels have been incidentally deepened by means of levees erected for protection against overflow. The bed of the Po in the neighborhood of Ponte Lagoscuro, where accurate data have been preserved, has been lowered one foot within the past century. The levees on the lower Thames were erected about 1767. By 1802 the channel depth between them had increased six feet.

The improvement to be expected from the maintenance of levees will be the result of an increase in the river's effective force as a whole. It will therefore be general in its character and gradual in development, and will not obviate the necessity of works placed in the channel to preserve its banks and cut down its bars. It is in connection with these, and as part of a complete and logical system of improvement, that they have their proper place.

An important distinction exists between the ordinary floods of an alluvial stream—that is, those which occur with a degree of regularity from year to year and its extraordinary floods, which occur only at irregular intervals. The former are part of the river's normal life; the latter are not. In the work of channel formation, the ordinary flood is the determining force. It is that by which and to which the river shapes its bed as nearly as it can. Therefore, if we can control and utilize the whole force of the ordinary flood in the work of channel improvement, we shall secure the benefit of all the normal energy of the river. The exceptional and abnormal floods may be disregarded. It follows that levees intended for the sole purpose of improving the channel may be of much less height than those intended for protection against overflow. For the latter purpose they should be able to restrain the greatest floods.

If any artificial additions to the banks of the Mississippi River are necessary to the improvement of its channel for purposes of navigation, it is the duty of the United States to provide them. That much is matter of national concern and national obligation. Protection against overflow is matter of domestic and individual concern, and therefore such levees as are necessary for that purpose should be provided by the communities interested. An ideal levee system would comprise two lines of embankment,--one of comparatively light character, following the river bank as closely as possible, and intended to restrain ordinary floods only ; the other a master dike, standing farther back, high and strong enough to withstand all floods, and following the general course of the river in long curves. But such a scheme is too vast for present consideration, to say nothing of the practical difficulty of its execution. And as long as one line of levee must stand at once for river improvement and land protection, the obvious suggestion of nature and justice is that the expense of it shall be divided between the States and the United States, according to its uses. To locate approximately the line dividing those uses is not beyond the possibilities of engineering. To devise measures by which a corresponding apportionment of burdens shall be made, and unity and effectiveness of control secured, ought not to be beyond the resources of patriotic statesmanship.

www.ingramcontent.com/pod-product-compliance
Lightning Source LLC
Chambersburg PA
CBHW021639270326
41931CB00008B/1089